The Twilight of Self-Reliance

Frontier Values and Contemporary America

WALLACE STEGNER

THE UNIVERSITY OF UTAH PRESS
Salt Lake City

Originally published in *The Tanner Lectures on Human Values,* vol. 2, edited by Sterling McMurrin. Copyright © 1981 by the Tanner Lectures on Human Values, a corporation

The Defiance House Man colophon is a registered trademark of the University of Utah Press. It is based upon a four-foot-tall, Ancient Puebloan pictograph (late PIII) near Glen Canyon, Utah.

12   11   10   09   08   1   2   3   4   5

Acknowledgments

Publication of this keepsake edition is made possible in part by
The Special Collections Department
J. Willard Marriott Library
by
The Tanner Lectures on Human Values
The Tanner Humanities Center
and by
The Wallace Stegner Center for Land, Resources, and the Environment
S. J. Quinney College of Law
The publisher gratefully acknowledges their generous support of this project.

Publisher's Note

Wallace Stegner (1909–1993) was born near Lake Mills, Iowa, and spent his childhood moving from place to place, including southwestern Canada, Montana, and even an orphanage in Seattle before his family finally settled in Salt Lake City, Utah. Stegner came to consider Salt Lake City his home town, having graduated from East High School and the University of Utah, and he has been embraced as a native son.

The high desert city established by Mormon pioneers and the landscapes that surround it were crucial to the development of Stegner's environmental ethic, and they helped to shape and inform such nonfiction as *Beyond the Hundredth Meridian: John Wesley Powell and the Second Opening of the West* (1954). The region also became the setting for three of his novels: *The Big Rock Candy Mountain* (1943), *Recapitulation* (1979), and *The Preacher and the Slave* (1950, later retitled *Joe Hill*). Throughout Stegner's life, Salt Lake City was a personal touchstone and a gateway to a wild but fragile world.

The occasions of the centennial of Wallace Stegner's birth on February 18, 1909, and the University of Utah Press's announcement of the Wallace Stegner Publication Prize in Environmental and American Western History, have provided the impetus for the re-publication of "The Twilight of Self-Reliance: Frontier Values and Contemporary America." Stegner originally delivered this Tanner Lecture at the University of Utah on February 25, 1980, and it appeared in volume two of the *Tanner Lectures on Human Values,* edited by Sterling McMurrin and published jointly by the Tanner Lectures on Human Values, Cambridge University Press, and the University of Utah Press. It is reprinted here as it appeared in that volume.

The University of Utah Press is pleased to make available this new keepsake edition of Stegner's lecture. We gratefully acknowledge the generous support of the Wallace Stegner Center for Land, Resources, and the Environment at the S. J. Quinney College of Law; the Special Collections Department of the J. Willard Marriott Library; and the Tanner Lectures on Human Values, all at the University of Utah, for their assistance in making this publication possible.

1

Henry David Thoreau was a philosopher not unwilling to criticize his country and his countrymen, but when he wrote the essay entitled "Walking" in 1862, at a time when his country was engaged in a desperate civil war, he wrote with what Mark Twain would have called the calm confidence of a Christian with four aces. He spoke America's stoutest self-confidence and most optimistic expectations. Eastward, he said, he walked only by force, but westward he walked free: he must walk toward Oregon and not toward Europe, and his trust in the future was total.

If the moon looks larger here than in Europe, probably the sun looks larger also. If the heavens of America appear infinitely higher, and the stars brighter, I trust that these facts are symbolical of the height to which the philosophy and poetry and religion of her inhabitants may one day soar. . . . I trust that we shall be more imaginative, that our thoughts will be clearer, fresher, and more ethereal, as our sky — our understanding more comprehensive and broader, like our plains — our intellect generally on a grander scale, like our thunder and lightning, our rivers and mountains and forests — and our hearts shall even correspond in breadth and depth and grandeur to our inland seas. Perchance there will appear to the traveler something, he knows not what, of *laeta* and *glabra*, of joyous and serene, in our very faces. Else to what end does the world go on, and why was America discovered?

The question was rhetorical; he knew the answer. To an American of his generation it was unthinkable that the greatest story in the history of civilized man — the finding and peopling of the New World — and the greatest opportunity since the Creation — the chance to remake men and their society into something cleansed of past mistakes, and closer to the heart's desire —

should end as one more betrayal of human credulity and hope.

Some moderns find that idea perfectly thinkable. Leslie Fiedler finds in the Montana Face, which whatever else it is is an authentically American one, not something joyous and serene, but the large vacuity of self-deluding myth. Popular books which attempt to come to grips with American values in these times walk neither toward Oregon nor toward Europe, but toward dead ends and jumping-off places. They bear such titles as *The Lonely Crowd*, *The Organization Man*, *Future Shock*, *The Culture of Narcissism*. This last, subtitled "American Life in an Age of Diminishing Expectations," reports "a way of life that is dying — the culture of competitive individualism, which in its decadence has carried the logic of individualism to the extreme of a war of all against all, the pursuit of happiness to the dead end of a narcissistic preoccupation with the self." It describes "a political system in which public lying has become endemic and routine," and a typical citizen who is haunted by anxiety and spends his time trying to find a meaning in his life. "His sexual attitudes are permissive rather than puritanical, even though his emancipation from ancient taboos brings him no sexual peace. . . . Acquisitive in the sense that his cravings have no limits, he does not accumulate goods and provisions against the future, in the manner of the acquisitive individualist of the nineteenth century political economy, but demands immediate gratification and lives in a state of restless, perpetually unsatisfied desire."

Assuming that Thoreau spoke for his time, as he surely did, and that Christopher Lasch speaks for at least elements and aspects of his, how did we get from there to here in little more than a century? Have the sturdiness of the American character and the faith in America's destiny that Thoreau took for granted been eroded entirely away? What happened to confidence, what happened to initiative and strenuousness and sobriety and responsibility, what happened to high purpose, what happened to hope? Are they gone, along with the Puritans' fear of pleasure? Was the American future, so clear in Thoreau's day, no more than a reflection of apparently unlimited resources, and does democracy dwindle along with the resources that begot it? Were we never really free, but only rich? In any event, if America was discovered only so that its citizens could pursue pleasure or grope for a meaning in their lives, then Thoreau and Lasch would be in agreement: Columbus should have stood at home.

Even if I knew answers, I could not detail them in an hour's lecture, or in a book. But since I believe that one of our most damaging American traits is our contempt for all history, including our own, I might spend an hour looking backward at what we were and how America changed us. A certain kind of modern American in the throes of an identity crisis is likely to ask, or bleat, "Who am I?" It might help him to find out who he started out to be, and having found that out, to ask himself if what he started out to be is still valid. And if most of what I touch on in this summary is sixth-grade American history, I do not apologize for that. History is not the proper midden for digging up novelties. Perhaps that is one reason why a nation bent on novelty ignores it. The obvious, especially the ignored obvious, is worth more than a Fourth of July or Bicentennial look.

2

Under many names — Atlantis, the Hesperides, Groenland, Brazillia, the Fortunate Isles — America was Europe's oldest dream. Found by Norsemen about the year 1000, it was lost again for half a millennium, and only emerged into reality at the beginning of the modern era, which we customarily date from the year 1500. There is even a theory, propounded by the historian Walter Webb in *The Great Frontier*, that the new world created the modern era — stimulated its birth, funded it, fueled it, fed it, gave it its impetus and direction and state of mind, formed its expectations and institutions, and provided it with a prosperity unexampled in history, a boom that lasted fully 400 years. If Professor Webb pushes his thesis a little hard, and if it has in it traces of the logical fallacy known as *post hoc, ergo propter hoc*, it still seems to me provocative and in some ways inescapable, and Webb seems entirely justified in beginning his discussion of America in medieval Europe. I shall do the same.

Pre-Columbian Europe, then. For 150 years it has been living close to the limit of its resources. It is always short of money, which means gold and silver, fiat money being still in the future. Its land is frozen in the structures of feudalism, owned by the crown, the church, and an aristocracy whose domains are shielded by laws of primogeniture and entail from sale or subdivision — from everything except the royal whim which gave, and can take away. Its food supply comes from sources that cannot be expanded, and its population, periodically reduced by the Black Death, is static or in decline. Peasants are bound to the soil, and both they and their masters are tied by feudal loyalties and obligations. Except among the powerful, individual freedom is not even a dream. Merchants, the guilds, and the middle class generally, struggle against the arrogance of the crown and an aristocracy dedicated to the anachronistic code of chivalry, which is often indistinguishable from brigandage. Faith is invested in a politicized, corrupt, but universal church just breaking up in the Reformation that will drown Europe in blood. Politics are a nest of snakes: ambitious nobles against ambitious kings, kings against pretenders and against each other, all of them trying to fill, by means of wars and strategic marriages, the periodic power vacuums created by the cracking of the Holy Roman Empire. The late Middle Ages still look on earthly life as a testing and preparation for the Hereafter. Fed on this opium, the little individual comes to expect his reward in heaven, or in the neck. Learning is just beginning to open out from scholastic rationalism into the empiricism of the Renaissance. Science, with all it will mean to men's lives and ways of thinking, has barely pipped its shell.

Out of this closed world Columbus sails in 1492 looking for

a new route to Asia, whose jewels and silks are coveted by Europe's elite, and whose spices are indispensable to nations with no means of preserving food except smoking and salting, and whose meat is often eaten high. The voyage of the three tiny ships is full of anxiety and hardship, but the end is miracle, one of those luminous moments in history: an after-midnight cry from the lookout on the *Pinta*, Columbus and his sailors crowding to the decks, and in the soft tropical night, by the light of a moon just past full, staring at a dark ambiguous shore and sniffing the perfumed breeze off an utterly new world.

Not Asia. Vasco da Gama will find one way to that, Magellan another. What Columbus has found is puzzling, of unknown size and unknown relation to anything. The imagination has difficulty taking it in. Though within ten years of Columbus' first voyage Vespucci will demonstrate that the Americas are clearly not Asia, Europe is a long time accepting the newness of the new world. Pedro de Castañeda, crossing the plains of New Mexico, Oklahoma, and Kansas with Coronado in 1541, is confident that they make one continuous land mass with China and Peru; and when Champlain sends Jean Nicolet to explore among the Nipissings on the way to Georgian Bay and the great interior lakes in 1635 — 133 years after Vespucci — Nicolet will take along in his bark canoe an embroidered mandarin robe, just in case, out on those wild rivers among those wild forests, he should come to the palace of the Great Khan and need ceremonial dress.

Understanding is a slow dawning, each exploration bringing a little more light. But when the dawn arrives, it is a blazing one. It finds its way through every door and illuminates every cellar and dungeon in Europe. Though the discovery of America is itself part of Europe's awakening, and results from purely European advances — foreshadowings of Copernican astronomy, a method for determining latitude, the development of the caravel and the lateen sail — the new world responds by accelerating every stir of curiosity, science, adventure, individualism, and hope in the old.

Because Europe has always dreamed westward, America, once realized, touches men's minds like fulfilled prophecy. It has lain out there in the gray wastes of the Atlantic, not only a continent waiting to be discovered, but a fable waiting to be agreed upon. It is not unrelated to the Hereafter. Beyond question, before it is half known, it will breed utopias and noble savages, fantasies of Perfection, New Jerusalems.

Professor Webb believes that to closed and limited Europe America came as a pure windfall, a once-in-the-history-of-the-world opportunity. Consider only one instance: the gold that Sir Francis Drake looted from Spanish galleons was the merest fragment of a tithe of what the Spaniards had looted from Mexico and Peru; and yet Queen Elizabeth out of her one-fifth royal share of the *Golden Hind*'s plunder was able to pay off the entire national debt of England and have enough left to help found the East India Company.

Perhaps, as Milton Friedman would insist, increasing the money supply only raised prices. Certainly American gold didn't help Europe's poor. It made the rich richer and kings more powerful and wars more implacable. Nevertheless, trickling outward from Spain as gift or expenditure, or taken from its ships by piracy, that gold affected all of Europe, stimulating trade and discovery, science, invention, everything that we associate with the unfolding of the Renaissance. It surely helped take European eyes off the Hereafter, and it did a good deal toward legitimizing the profit motive. And as the French and English, and to a lesser extent the Dutch and Swedes, began raiding America, other and more substantial riches than gold flooded back: new food plants, especially Indian corn and the potato, which revolutionized eating habits and brought on a steep rise in population that lasted more than a century; furs; fish from the swarming Newfoundland banks, especially important to countries still largely Catholic; tobacco for the indulgence of a fashionable new habit; timber for ships and masts; sugar and rum from the West Indies.

Those spoils alone might have rejuvenated Europe. But there was something else, at first not valued or exploited, that eventually would lure Europeans across the Atlantic and transform them. The most revolutionary gift of the new world was land itself, and the independence and aggressiveness that land ownership meant. Land, unoccupied and unused except by savages who in European eyes did not count, land available to anyone with the initiative to take it, made America, Opportunity, and Freedom synonymous terms.

But only later. The early comers were raiders, not settlers. The first Spanish towns were beachheads from which to scour the country for treasure, the first French settlements on the St. Lawrence were beachheads of the fur trade. Even the English on Roanoke Island, and later at Jamestown, though authentic settlers, were hardly pioneers seeking the promised land. Many were bond servants and the scourings of debtors' prisons. They did not come, they were sent. Their hope of working off their bondage and starting new in a new country was not always rewarded, either. Bruce and William Catton estimate that eight out of ten indentured servants freed to make new lives in America failed — returned to pauperism, or became the founders of a poor-white class, or died of fevers trying to compete with black slaves on tobacco or sugar plantations, or turned outlaw.

Nevertheless, for the English who at Jamestown and Plymouth and the Massachusetts Bay Colony began to take ownership of American land in the early seventeenth century, land was the transfiguring gift. The historian who remarked that the entire history of the United States could be read in terms of real estate was not simply making words.

Here was an entire continent which, by the quaint assumptions of the raiders, was owned by certain absentee crowned heads whose subjects had made the first symbolic gesture of claiming it. They had rowed a boat into a rivermouth, sighted and named a cape, raised a cross on a beach, buried a brass plate, or harangued a crowd of bewildered Indians. Therefore Ferdinand and Isabella, or Elizabeth, or Louis owned from that point to the farthest boundary in every direction. But land without people was valueless. The Spaniards imported the *encomienda* system — that is, transplanted feudalism — and used the Indians as peons. The French built only forts at which to collect the wilderness wealth of furs. But the English were another kind, and they were the ones who created the American pattern.

"Are you ignorant of the difference between the king of England and the king of France?" Duquesne asked the Iroquois in the 1750's. "Go see the forts that our king has established and you will see that you can still hunt under their very walls . . . . The English, on the contrary, are no sooner in possession of a place than the game is driven away. The forest falls before them as they advance, and the soil is laid bare so that you can scarce find the wherewithal to erect a shelter for the night."

To be made valuable, land must be sold cheap or given away to people who would work it, and out of that necessity was born a persistent American expectation. The very word "claim" that we came to use for a parcel of land reflected our feeling that free or cheap land was a right, and that the land itself was a commodity. The Virginia Company and Lord Calvert both tried to encourage landed estates on the English pattern, and both failed because in America men would not work land unless they owned it, and would not be tied to a proprietor's acres when they could go off into the woods and have any land they wanted, simply for the taking. Their claim might not be strictly legal, but it often held: hence the development of what came to be known as squatters' rights. As Jefferson would later write in *Notes on Virginia*, Europe had an abundance of labor and a dearth of land, America an abundance of land and a dearth of labor. That made all the difference. The opportunity to own land not only freed men, it made labor honorable and opened up the future to hope and the possibility of independence, perhaps of a fortune.

The consequences inform every notion we have of ourselves. Admittedly there were all kinds of people in early America, as there are all kinds in our time — saints and criminals, dreamers and drudges, pushers and con men. But the new world did something similar to all of them. Of the most energetic ones it made ground-floor capitalists; out of nearly everyone it leached the last traces of servility. Cut off from control, ungoverned and virtually untaxed, people learned to resent the imposition of authority, even that which they had created for themselves. Dependent on their own strength and ingenuity in a strange land, they learned to dismiss tradition and old habit, or rather, simply forgot them. Up in Massachusetts the idea of the equality of souls before God probably helped promote the idea of earthly equality; the notion of a personal covenant with God made the way easier for social and political agreements such as the Plymouth Compact and eventually the Constitution of the United States. In the observed freedom of the Indian from formal government there may have been a dangerous example for people who had lived under governments notably unjust and oppressive. Freedom itself forced the creation not only of a capitalist economy based on land, but of new forms of social contract. When thirteen loosely-allied colonies made common cause against the mother country, the League of the Iroquois may well have provided one model of confederation.

"The rich stay in Europe," wrote Hector St. John de Crèvecoeur before the Revolution. "It is only the middling and poor that emigrate." Middle class values emigrated with them, and middle class ambitions. Resentment of aristocrats and class distinctions accompanied the elevation of the work ethic. Hardship, equal opportunity to rise, the need for common defense against the Indians, and the necessity for all to postpone the rewards of labor brought the English colonists to nearly the same level and imbued all but the retarded and the most ne'er-do-well with the impulse of upward mobility. And if the practical need to hew a foothold out of the continent left many of them unlettered and ignorant, that deficiency, combined with pride, often led to the disparagement of cultivation and the cultivated as effete and European. Like work, barbarism and boorishness tended to acquire status, and in some parts of America still retain it.

Land was the base, freedom the consequence. Not even the little parochial tyranny of the Puritans in Massachusetts could be made to stick indefinitely. In fact, the Puritans' chief objection to Roger Williams, when they expelled him, was not his unorthodoxy but his declaration that the Colonists had no right to their lands, the king not having had the right to grant them in the first place. Williams also expressed an early pessimistic view of the American experiment that clashed with prevailing assumptions and forecast future disillusion. "The common trinity of the world — Profit, Preferment, and Pleasure — will be here the tria omnia, as in all the world besides . . . and God Land will be as great a God with us English as God Gold was with the Spaniard." A sour prophet indeed — altogether too American in his dissenting opinions and his challenging of authority. And right besides. No wonder they chased him off to Rhode Island.

Students of the Revolution have wondered whether it was really British tyranny that lit rebellion, or simply American outrage at the imposition of even the mildest imperial control after decades of benign neglect. Certainly one of George III's worst blunders was his 1763 decree forbidding settlement beyond the crest of the Alleghenies. That was worse than the Stamp Act or the Navigation Acts, for land speculators were already sniffing the western wind. When Daniel Boone took settlers over the Cumberland Gap in 1775 he was working for speculators. George Washington and Benjamin Franklin, who had a good deal to do with the Revolution, both had interests in western land. Only a very revisionist historian would call our revolution a real estate rebellion, a revolt of the subdividers, but it did have that aspect.

And very surely, as surely as the endless American forests put a curve in the helves of the axes that chopped them down, the continent worked on those who settled it. From the first frontiers in Virginia and Massachusetts through all the successive frontiers that, as Jefferson said, required Americans to start fresh every generation, America was in the process of creating a democratic, energetic, practical, profit-motivated society that resembled Europe less and less as it worked westward. At the same time, it was creating the complicated creature we spent our first century as a nation learning to recognize and trying to define: the American.

3

"Who then is the American, this new man?" asked Crèvecoeur, and answered his own question in a book published in 1782 as *Letters from an American Farmer.* We were, he said, a nation of cultivators; and it was the small farmer, the independent, frugal, hard-working, self-respecting freeholder, that he idealized — the same yeoman farmer that only a little later Jefferson would call the foundation of the republic. But out on the fringes of settlement Crèvecoeur recognized another type. Restless, migratory, they lived as much by hunting as by farming, for protecting their crops and stock against wild animals put the gun in their hands, and "once hunters, farewell to the plough. The chase renders them ferocious, gloomy, and unsocial"; they exhibit "a strange sort of lawless profligacy"; and their children, having no models except their parents, "grow up a mongrel breed, half civilized, half savage."

Crèvecoeur, familiar only with the eastern seaboard, thought the frontiersman already superseded almost everywhere by the more sober and industrious farmer. He could not know that on farther frontiers beyond the Appalachians, beyond the Mississippi, beyond the Missouri and the Rocky Mountains, the breed would renew itself for another hundred years, repeating over and over the experience that had created it in the first place. The Revolutionary War was only the climax of the American Revolution, which was the most radical revolution in history because it started from scratch, from wilderness, and repeated that beginning over and over.

The pioneer farmer has a respectable place in our tradition and an equally respectable place in our literature, from Cooper's *The Pioneers* to Rölvaag's *Giants in the Earth*. But it was the border hunter who captured our imaginations and became a myth. He was never a soft or necessarily attractive figure. Ferocious he always was, gloomy often, antisocial by definition. As D. H. Lawrence and a whole school of critics have pointed out, he was a loner, often symbolically an orphan, strangely sexless (though more in literature than in fact), and a killer. We know him not only from the Boones, Crocketts, Carsons, and Bridgers of history, but from Cooper's Leatherstocking and all his literary descendants. His most memorable recent portrait is Boone Caudill in A. B. Guthrie's *Big Sky*, who most appropriately heads for the mountains and a life of savage freedom after a murderous fight with his father. Most appropriately, for according to Lawrence's *Studies in Classic American Literature*, one essential symbolic act of the American is the murder of Father Europe, and another is re-baptism in the wilderness.

We may observe those symbolic acts throughout our tradition, in a hundred variations from the crude and barbarous to the highly sophisticated. Emerson was performing them in such essays as "Self-Reliance" ("Trust thyself: every heart vibrates to that iron string") and "The American Scholar" ("We have listened too long to the courtly muses of Europe"). Whitman sent them as a barbaric yawp over the rooftops of the world. Thoreau spoke them in the quotation with which I began this lecture, and put them into practice in his year on Walden Pond.

The virtues of the frontiersman, real or literary, are Indian virtues, warrior qualities of bravery, endurance, stoical indifference to pain and hardship, recklessness, contempt for law, a hawk-like need of freedom. Often in practice an outlaw, the frontiersman in literature is likely to display a certain noble savagery, a degree of natural goodness that has a more sophisticated parallel in the common American delusion, shared even by Jefferson, who should have known better, that untutored genius is more to be admired than genius schooled. In the variants of the frontiersman that Henry Nash Smith traces in *Virgin Land* — in flatboatman, logger, cowboy, miner, in literary and mythic figures from the Virginian to the Lone Ranger and Superman — the Indian qualities persist, no matter how overlaid with comedy or occupational detail. Malcolm Cowley has shown how they emerge in a quite different sort of literature in the stiff-upper-lip code hero of Ernest Hemingway.

We need not admire them wholeheartedly in order to recognize them in their modern forms. They put the Winchesters on the gunracks of pickups and the fury into the arguments of the gun lobby. They dictate the leather of Hell's Angels and the whanged buckskin of drugstore Carsons. Our most ruthless industrial, financial, and military buccaneers have displayed them. The Sagebrush Rebellion and those who would open Alaska to a final stage of American continent-busting adopt them as a platform. Without them there would have been no John Wayne movies. At least as much as the sobriety and self-reliant industry of the pioneer farmer, it is the restlessness and intractability of the frontiersman that drives our modern atavists away from civilization into the woods and deserts, there to build their yurts and geodesic domes and live self-reliant lives with no help except from trust funds, unemployment insurance, and food stamps.

This mythic figure lasts. He is a model of conduct of many kinds. He directs our fantasies. Curiously, in almost all his historic forms he is both landless and destructive, his kiss is the kiss of death. The hunter roams the wilderness but owns none of it. As Daniel Boone, he served the interests of speculators and capitalists; even as Henry David Thoreau he ended his life as a surveyor of town lots. As mountain man he was virtually a bond servant to the company, and his indefatigable labors all but eliminated the beaver and undid all the conservation work of beaver engineering. The logger achieved his roughhouse liberty within the constraints of a brutally punishing job whose result was the enrichment of great capitalist families such as the Weyerhausers and the destruction of most of the magnificent American forests. The cowboy, so mythically free in books and movies, was a hired man on horseback, a slave to cows and the deadliest enemy of the range he used to ride.

Do these figures represent our wistful dream of freedom from the shackles of family and property? Probably they do. It may be important to note that it is the mountain man, logger, and cowboy whom we have made into myths, not the Astors and General Ashleys, the Weyerhausers, or the cattle kings. The lowlier figures, besides being more democratic and so matching the folk image better, may incorporate a dream not only of freedom but of irresponsibility. In any case, any variety of the frontiersman is more attractive to modern Americans than is the responsible, pedestrian, hard-working pioneer farmer breaking his back in a furrow to achieve ownership of his claim and give his children a start in the world. The freedom of the frontiersman is a form of mortal risk and contains the seed of its own destruction. The shibboleth of this breed is prowess.

The pioneer farmer is another matter. He had his own forms of self-reliance; he was a mighty coper, but his freedom of movement was restricted by family and property, and his shibboleth was not prowess but growth. He put off the present in favor of the future. Travelers on the Midwestern frontier during the 1820's, 30's, and 40's were universally moved to amazement at how farms, villages, even cities, had risen magically where only a few years before bears had been measuring their reach on the trunks of trees. British travelers such as Mrs. Trollope found the pioneer farms primitive, the towns crude, and the brag of the townsmen offensive, but Americans such as Timothy Flint, Thomas Nuttall, and John James Audubon regarded the settlement of the Midwest with a pride that was close to awe. Mormons looking back on their communal miracles in Nauvoo and Salt Lake City feel that same pride. Progress we have always measured quantitatively, in terms of acres plowed, turnpikes graded, miles of railroad built, bridges and canals constructed. I heard former Governor Pat Brown of California chortle with delight when the word came that California had passed New York in the population race. All through our history we have had the faith that growth is good, and bigger is better.

And here we may observe a division, a fault-line, in American feeling. Cooper had it right in *The Pioneers* nearly 160 years ago. Leatherstocking owns Cooper's imagination, but the town builders own the future, and Leatherstocking has to give way. *The Pioneers* is at once an exuberant picture of the breaking of the wilderness and a lament for its passing; and it is as much the last of the frontiersmen as the last of the Mohicans that the Leatherstocking series mourns. Many of Cooper's successors have felt the same way — hence the elegiac tone of so many of our novels of the settlement and the land. We hear it in Willa Cather's *A Lost Lady*, where the railroad builder Captain Forrester is so much larger than anyone in the shrunken present. We hear it in Larry McMurtry's *Horseman, Pass By*, which before it was made into the movie *Hud* was a requiem for the old-time cattleman. A country virtually without history and with no regard for history — history is bunk, said Henry Ford — exhibits an odd mournfulness over the passing of its brief golden age.

The romantic figure of the frontiersman was doomed to pass with the wilderness that made him. He was essentially over by the 1840's, though in parts of the West he lingered on as an anachronism. His epitaph was read, as Frederick Jackson Turner noted in a famous historical essay, by the census of 1890, which found no continuous line of frontier existing anywhere in the United States. He was not the only one who died of that census report. The pioneer farmer died too, for without a frontier there was no more free land. But whether the qualities that the frontier had built into both frontiersman and farmer died when the line of settlement withered at the edge of the shortgrass plains — that is not so clear.

4

Not only was free land gone by 1890, or at least any free land capable of settlement, but by the second decade of the twentieth century the population of the United States, despite all the empty spaces in the arid West, had reached the density which historians estimate congested Europe had had in 1500. The growth that Jefferson had warned against had gone on with astounding speed. The urban poor of Europe whose immigration he would have discouraged had swamped the original nation of mainly-Protestant, mainly–North European origins, and together with the industrial revolution, accelerated by the Civil War, had created precisely the sort of manufacturing nation, complete with urban slums and urban discontents, that he had feared. We were just at the brink of changing over from the nation of cultivators that Crèvecoeur had described and Jefferson advocated into an industrial nation dominated by corporations and capitalistic buccaneers still unchecked by any social or political controls.

The typical American was not a self-reliant and independent landowner, but a wage earner; and the victory of the Union in the Civil War had released into the society millions of former slaves whose struggle to achieve full citizenship was sure to trouble the waters of national complacency for a century and perhaps much longer. The conditions that had given us freedom and opportunity and optimism were over, or seemed to be. We were entering the era of the muckrakers, and we gave them plenty of muck to rake. And even by 1890 the note of disenchantment, the gloomy Dostoyevskyan note that William Dean Howells said did not belong in American literature, which should deal with the more smiling aspects of life, had begun to make its way into our novels.

After 1890 we could ask ourselves in increasing anxiety the question that Thoreau had asked rhetorically in 1862. To what end *did* the world go on, and why *was* America discovered? Had the four hundred years of American experience created anything new, apart from some myths as remote as Romulus and Remus, or were we back in the unbreakable circle from which Columbus had sprung us?

From 1890 to the present there have been plenty of commentators, with plenty of evidence on their side, to say that indeed we have slipped back into that vicious circle; and when we examine the products of the Melting Pot we find lugubrious reminders that it has not melted everybody down into any sort of standard American. What we see instead is a warring melee of minority groups — racial, ethnic, economic, sexual, linguistic — all claiming their right to the American standard without surrendering the cultural identities that make them still unstandard. We seem to be less a nation than a collection of what current cant calls "communities": the Black Community, the Puerto Rican Community, the Chicano Community, the Chinese Community, the Gay Community, the Financial Community, the Academic Community, and a hundred others. We seem to approach not the standard product of the Melting Pot but the mosaic that Canadians look forward to, and that they think will save them from becoming the stereotypes they think we are.

With all respect to Canada, we are not a set of clones. We are the wildest mixture of colors, creeds, opinions, regional differences, occupations, and types. Nor is Canada the permanent mosaic it says it wants to be. Both nations, I am convinced, move with glacial slowness toward that unity in diversity, that *e pluribus unum* of a North American synthesis, that is inevitable, or nearly so, no matter which end it is approached from. When we arrive there, a century or two or three hence, darker of skin and more united in mind, the earlier kind of American who was shaped by the frontier will still be part of us — of each of us, even if our ancestors came to this continent after the frontier as a fact was gone.

For as Turner pointed out, the repeated experience of the frontier through more than two hundred and fifty years coalesced gradually into a package of beliefs, habits, faiths, assumptions, and values, and these values in turn gave birth to laws and institutions that have had a continuous shaping effect on every newer American who enters the society either by birth or immigration. These are the things that bind us together no matter how many other forces may be pushing us apart. Language is one thing. I believe it has to be English, for language is at the core of every culture and inseparable from its other manifestations. If we permit bilingualism or multilingualism more than temporarily as an aid to assimilation, we will be balkanized and undone, as Canada is in danger of being by the apparently irremediable division between the Anglophones and the Francophones. The Bill of Rights is another unifier. We rely on it daily — even our enemies rely on it. And the images of ourselves, including the variant myths, that we developed when we were a younger, simpler, and more hopeful nation are still another. The national character, diffuse or not, recognizable if not definable, admirable and otherwise, bends newcomers to its image and outlasts time, change, crowding, shrinking resources, and fashionable pessimism. It has bent those apparently untouched by the Melting Pot, bent them more than they may know. Thus James Baldwin, visiting Africa, discovered to his surprise that though black, he was no African: he was an American, and thought and felt like one.

Time makes slow changes in our images of ourselves, but at their best, the qualities our writers and mythmakers have perpetuated are worth our imitation. The untutored decency and mongrel smartness of Huckleberry Finn, as well as the dignity that the slave Jim salvaged out of an oppressed life, could only have been imagined in America. The innocent philistinism of Howells' Silas Lapham could have been imagined by a European observer, but the ethical worth that nearly ennobles Lapham in his financial crisis is — realistic or not — pure American. Henry James's American, significantly named Christopher Newman, has a magnanimity that matches his naïveté. And the literary archetypes of the pre-1890 period are not the only ones. We have had political leaders who have represented us in more than political ways, and two at least who have taught us at the highest level who we are and who we might be.

Washington I could never get next to; he is a noble impersonal obelisk on the Mall. But Jefferson and Lincoln are something else. Jefferson did more than any other man to shape this democracy: formulated its principles in the Declaration of Independence and insisted on the incorporation of the Bill of Rights into the Constitution; had a hand in preventing the establishment of a state church; created the monetary system; framed the rules for the government of the western territories; invented the pattern for the survey of the public domain; bought Louisiana; sent Lewis and Clark to the western ocean and back, thus fathering one of our most heroic legends and inventing Manifest Destiny. If he had a clouded love affair with the slave half-sister of his dead wife, that only winds him more tightly into the ambiguous history of his country. As for Lincoln, he gave eloquence and nobility to the homespun values of frontier democracy. He was native mind and native virtue at their highest reach, and he too, like Jefferson but more sternly, was mortally entangled in the slave question that threatened to break America apart before it came of age.

Historians in these anti-heroic times have sometimes scolded the folk mind for apotheosizing Jefferson and Lincoln; and certainly, from their temples on the Potomac, they do brood over our national life like demigods. But as Bernard DeVoto said in one of his stoutly American "Easy Chairs," the folk mind is often wiser than the intellectuals. It knows its heroes and clings to them stubbornly even when heroes are out of fashion. Unfortunately, it is about as unreliable in its choice of heroes as in its creation of myths. It has a dream of jackpots as well as a dream of moral nobility and political freedom; it can make a model for imitation out of Jim Fisk or a myth out of a psychopathic killer like Billy the Kid almost as readily as it makes them out of the Great Emancipator.

5

These days, young people do not stride into their future with the confidence their grandparents knew. Over and over, in recent years, I have heard the cold undertone of doubt and uncertainty when I talk with college students. The American Dream has suffered distortion and attrition; for many, it is a dream glumly awakened from.

Per Hansa, in *Giants in the Earth*, could homestead Dakota farmland, gamble his strength against nature, lose his life in the struggle, but win in the end by handing down a productive farm to his son, and insuring him a solid, self-respecting place in the world. Per Hansa's grandsons have no such chances. Only one of them can inherit the family farm, for it would not be an economic unit if divided (it barely is while still undivided), and so something like primogeniture must be invoked to protect it. The other sons cannot hope to buy farms of their own. Land is too high, money is too expensive, machinery is too costly. The products of a farm acquired on those terms could not even pay the interest on the debt. So the other sons have a choice between leaving the farm, which they know and like, and going into the job market; or hiring out as tenant farmers or hired hands to some factory in the field. All over the United States, for several decades, farms have become fewer, larger, and more mechanized, and family ownership has grown less. Though I have no statistics in the matter, I would not be surprised to hear before the end of the 1980's that investors from the Middle East, Hong Kong, and Japan own as much American farmland as independent American farmers do.

For the vast majority of American youth who are not farmers, the options of independence have likewise shrunk. What they have to consider, more likely than not, is a job — a good job, in a company with a good pay scale, preferably, and with guaranteed promotions and a sound retirement plan. The future is not a thing we want to risk; when possible, we insure against it. And for the economically disadvantaged, the core-city youth, the minorities ethnic or otherwise, the people with inferior capacities or bad training or no luck, it is as risky as it ever was in frontier times, but without the promise it used to hold, and with no safety valve such as free land used to provide.

So we return to the vision of Christopher Lasch in *The Culture of Narcissism*. With some of it, especially its glib Freudian analyses of straw men, I am not in sympathy. By some parts, even when I think accurate observations are being marshaled to a dubious conclusion, I have to be impressed. The vision is apocalyptic. Lasch sees our cities as bankrupt or ungovernable or both, our political life corrupt, our bureaucracies greedy and expanding, our great corporations pervaded by the dog-eat-dog individualism of managerial ambition, maximized profits, and "business ethics" — which bear the same relation to ethics that military intelligence bears to intelligence. He sees Americans degraded by selfishness, cynicism, and venality, religion giving way to therapy and lunatic cults, education diluted by the no-fail concept, high school graduates unable to sign their names, family life shattered and supervision of children increasingly passed on to courts, clinics, or the state. He sees sexuality rampant, love extinct, work avoided, instant pleasure pursued as the whole aim of life. He sees excellence disparaged because our expectations so far exceed our deserving that any real excellence is a threat. He sees the Horatio Alger hero replaced in the American Pantheon by the Happy Hooker, the upright sportsmanship of Frank Merriwell replaced by the sports manners of John McEnroe, and all the contradictory strains of American life beginning to focus in the struggle between a Far Right asserting frontier ruthlessness and unhampered free enterprise, and a welfare liberalism to which even the requirement of reading English in order to vote may seem like a violation of civil rights.

The culture hero of Lasch's America is no Jefferson or Lincoln, no Leatherstocking or Carson, no Huck Finn or Silas Lapham. He is no hero at all, but the limp, whining anti-hero of Joseph Heller's *Something Happened* — self-indulgent, sneaky, scared of his superiors, treacherous to his inferiors, held together only by clandestine sex and by a sticky sentiment for the children to whom he has given nothing, the wife whom he ignores and betrays, and the mother whom he filed away in a nursing home and forgot.

Not quite what Thoreau predicted. The question is — and it is a question forced by Lasch's implication that his generalizations, and Heller's character, speak for the whole culture — does the Lasch–Heller characteristic American match the Americans you know in Salt Lake City and I know in California and other people know in Omaha and Des Moines and Wichita and Dallas and Hartford and Bangor?

I doubt that we know many such limp dishrags as Heller's Bob Slocum, but we recognize elements of the world he lives in. We have watched the progress of the sexual revolution and the one-hoss-shay collapse of the family. We have observed how, in the mass media and hence in the popular imagination, celebrity has crowded out distinction. We have seen the gap widen between rich and poor, have seen crime push itself into high places and make itself all but impregnable, have watched the drug culture work outward from the ghettos into every level of American life. We are not unaware of how the Pleasure Principle, promoted about equally by prosperity, advertisers, and a certain kind of therapist, has eaten the pilings out from under dedication and accomplishment; how we have given up saving for the future and started spending for the present, because the Pleasure Principle preaches gratification, because the tax laws and inflation discourage saving and encourage borrowing. We have stood by uneasily while the Pleasure Principle invaded the schools, and teachers tried desperately to save something out of the wreck by pretending to be entertainers. Johnny can't read, but he expects his English class to be as entertaining as an X-rated movie. Increasingly he seems to be a vessel which dries out and deteriorates if it is not kept filled, and so for his leisure hours he must have a four-hundred-dollar stereo and/or a color TV, and when he walks around he carries a transistor radio, tuned loud. If he doesn't get a ski weekend during the winter term, he calls a school strike. He has never worn a tie, but he can vote, being eighteen.

We have lived through times when it has seemed that everything ran downhill, when great corporations were constantly being caught in bribery, price fixing, or the dumping of chemical wastes in the public's backyard — when corporate liberty, in other words, was indulged at the public expense. We have seen the proliferation of government bureaus, some of them designed to curb corporate abuses and some apparently designed only to inhibit the freedom of citizens. We have watched some of our greatest cities erupt in mindless violence. We have built ourselves a vast industrial trap in which, far from being the self-reliant individuals we once were, and still are in fantasy, we are absolutely helpless when the power fails.

Can any of the values left over from the frontier speak persuasively to the nation we have become? Some of the most antisocial of them still do, especially the ruthless go-getterism of an earlier phase of capitalism. Single-minded dedication, self-reliance, a willingness to work long and hard persist most visibly not in the average democratic individual but in the managers of exploitative industry and in spokesmen for the Far Right. Expressed in a modern context, they inspire not admiration but repulsion, they make us remember that some of the worst things we have done to our continent, our society, and our character have been done under their auspices. We remain a nation of real estate operators, trading increasingly small portions of the increasingly overburdened continent back and forth at increasingly inflated prices.

But I have a faith that, however obscured and overlooked, other tendencies remain from our frontier time. In spite of multiplying crises, galloping inflation, energy shortages, a declining dollar, shaken confidence, crumbling certainties, we cannot know many Americans without perceiving stubborn residues of toughness, ingenuity, and cheerfulness. The American is far less antisocial than he used to be; he has had to learn social values as he created them. Outside of business, where he still has a great deal to learn, he is very often such a human being as the future would be safe with.

I recognize Heller's Bob Slocum as one kind of contemporary American, but I do not commonly meet him in my own life. The kind I do meet may be luckier than most, but he seems to me far more representative than Bob Slocum, and I have met him all over the country and among most of the shifting grades of American life. He is likely to work reasonably hard, but not kill himself working; he doesn't have to, whether he is an electronics plant manager or a professor or a bricklayer. If he is still an individualist in many ways, he is also a belonger. If he belongs to a minority he is probably a civil rights activist, or at least sympathizer. If he belongs to that group of "middle Americans" about whom Robert Coles wrote a perceptive book, he may be confused and shaken by some equal-opportunity developments, but as often as not he understands the historical context and the necessity for increasing the access to opportunity, and if not supportive, is at least acquiescent.

He has not given up the future, as Lasch believes. He is often very generous. He gives to good causes, or causes he thinks good, and in a uniquely American way he associates himself with others in ad hoc organizations to fight for better schools, more parks, political reforms, social justice. That is the remote but unmistakable echo of the Plymouth Compact — government improvised for the occasion; government of, by, and for the people.

This American may be pinched, but he is not poor by any definition. He is lower middle, middle middle, upper middle. Whether he works for a corporation, a university, a hospital, a government bureau, whether he is a skilled laborer or a professional, he has a considerable stake in this society. He is always respectful of money, but he cannot be called money-crazy: money-craziness occurs much more commonly among the poor who have far too little or the rich who have far too much. Unless he is financially involved in growth, in which case he may be everything I have just said he is not, he is wary of uncontrolled growth and even opposed to it. Free enterprise in the matter of real estate speculation strikes him as more often fruitful of social ill than social good, just as industrialization strikes him not as the cure for our ills but the cause of many of them. He takes his pleasures and relaxations, and expects far more of them than his frontier grandparents did, but he can hardly be called a pleasure freak bent on instant gratification. He is capable, as many of us observed during a recent California drouth, of abstinence and economy and personal sacrifice in the public interest, and would be capable of much more of those if he had leaders who encouraged them.

This sort of American is either disregarded or disparaged in the alarming books that assay our culture. Lasch, though he would like him better than the kind he describes, seems to think him gone past retrieval. But Lasch, like some other commentators, is making a point and selects his evidence. To some extent also, he makes the New Yorker mistake of mistaking New York for the United States. To an even greater extent he reads a certain class as if it were a cross section of the entire population. He would honestly like to get us back onto the tracks he thinks we have left, or onto new tracks that lead somewhere, and he deplores what he sees as much as anyone would.

But in fact we may be more on the tracks than he believes we are. His book is rather like the books of captious British travelers in the first half of the nineteenth century. Not having experienced the potency of the dream of starting from scratch, he sees imperfections as failures, not as stages of a long slow effort. But there is something very American about *The Culture of Narcissism*, too. We have always had a habit, when we were not bragging, of accepting Father Europe's view that we are short on cultural finesse and that our fabled moral superiority is a delusion. It may *be* a delusion; that does not make an American a creature unworthy of study, or American society a dismal failure. We have never given up the habit we acquired while resisting George III: we knock government and authority, including our own; we badmouth ourselves; like Robert Frost's liberal, we won't take our own side in an argument.

It is time we did. In 1992, twelve years from now, it will be half a millennium since Columbus and his sailors poured out on deck to see the new world. In half a millennium we should have gone at least part way toward what we started out to be. In spite of becoming the dominant world power, the dominant industrial as well as agricultural nation, the dominant force for freedom in the world, in spite of the fact that historically our most significant article of export has been the principle of liberty, in spite of the fact that the persecuted and poor of the earth still look to the United States as their haven and their hope — ask a Mexican wetback family, ask a family of Vietnamese boat people — many of us have never quite got it straight what it was we started out to be, and some of us have forgotten.

Habits change with time, but the principles have not changed. We remain a free and self-reliant people and a land of opportunity, and if our expectations are not quite what they once were, they are still greater expectations than any people in the world can indulge. A little less prosperity might be good for some of us, and I think we can confidently expect God to provide what we need. We could also do with a little less pleasure, learn to limit it in quantity and upgrade it in quality. Like money, pleasure is an admirable by-product and a contemptible goal. That lesson will still take some learning.

Give us time. Half a millennium is not enough. Give us time to wear out the worst of the selfishness and greed and turn our energy to humane and socially useful purposes. Give us a perennial few (a few is all any society can expect, and all any society really needs) who do not forget the high purpose that marked our beginnings, and Thoreau may yet be proved right in his prophecy.

Above all, let us not forget or mislay our optimism about the possible. In all our history we have never been more than a few years without a crisis, and some of those crises, the Civil War for one, and the whole problem of slavery, have been graver and more alarming than our present one. We have never stopped criticizing the performance of our elected leaders, and we have indeed had some bad ones and have survived them. The system was developed by accident and opportunity, but it is a system of extraordinary resilience. The United States has a ramshackle government, Robert Frost told Khrushchev in a notable conversation. The more you ram us, the harder we shackle. In the midst of our anxiety we should remember that this is the oldest and stablest republic in the world. Whatever its weaknesses and failures, we show no inclination to defect. The currents of defection flow the other way.

Let us not forget who we started out to be, or be surprised that we have not yet arrived. Robert Frost can again, as so often, be our spokesman. "The land was ours before we were the land's," he wrote. "Something we were withholding made us weak, until we found that it was ourselves we were withholding from our land of living." He was a complex, difficult, often malicious man, with grave faults. He was also one of our great poets, as much in the American grain as Lincoln or Thoreau. He contained within himself many of our most contradictory qualities, he never learned to subdue his selfish personal demon —

and he was never a favorite of the New York critics, who thought him a country bumpkin.

But like the folk mind, he was wiser than the intellectuals. No American was ever wiser. Listening to him, we can refresh ourselves with our own best image, and renew our vision of America: not as Perfection, not as Heaven on Earth, not as New Jerusalem, but as flawed glory and exhilarating task.